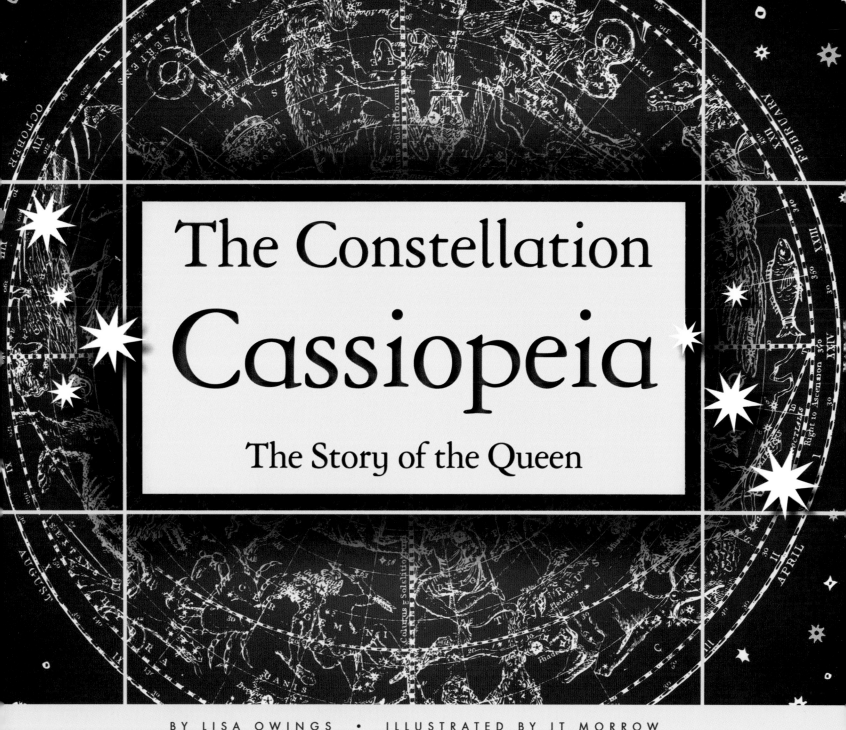

The Constellation
Cassiopeia

The Story of the Queen

BY LISA OWINGS • ILLUSTRATED BY JT MORROW

The Child's World

Published by The Child's World®
1980 Lookout Drive • Mankato, MN 56003-1705
800-599-READ • www.childsworld.com

Acknowledgments
The Child's World®: Mary Berendes, Publishing Director
Red Line Editorial: Editorial direction and production
The Design Lab: Design

Photographs ©: US Naval Observatory Library, 5; SOHO (ESA &
NASA), 6; Linda Brotkorb/Shutterstock Images, 7; NASA/JPL-Caltech/
STScI/CXC/SAO, 9 (top); John A Davis/Shutterstock Images, 9 (bottom);
ARCHITECTE/Shutterstock Images, 11; Arpad Benedek/iStockphoto, 12;
OPIS Zagreb/Shutterstock Images, 13; Library of Congress, 14; Duncan
Walker/iStockphoto, 17; Yousuf Khan/iStockphoto, 26; TAO Images
Limited/Getty Images, 27

Design elements: Alisafoytik/Dreamstime

ISBN: 9781623234843
LCCN: 2013931330

Printed in the United States of America
Mankato, MN
July, 2013
PA02168

ABOUT THE AUTHOR

Lisa Owings has a degree in English and creative writing from the University of Minnesota. She has written and edited a wide variety of educational books for young people. Lisa lives in Andover, Minnesota, where she can see Cassiopeia every night.

ABOUT THE ILLUSTRATOR

JT Morrow has worked as a freelance illustrator for more than 20 years and has won several awards. He also works in graphic design and animation. Morrow lives just south of San Francisco, California, with his wife and daughter.

Table of Contents

CHAPTER 1

The Constellation Cassiopeia

The night sky is like a window to the **universe**. Through it you can see the stars shining brightly in the darkness. People have always wondered about the stars. How did they come to be hung in the sky? People have also traced pictures with the stars. The groups of stars that form the pictures are called constellations. And the constellations tell wonderful stories. One of these stories is about a lovely but **vain** queen. The ancient Greeks gave her the name Cassiopeia (kah-see-ah-PEE-ah).

▶ Opposite page: Cassiopeia sits on her throne in the night sky.

Cassiopeia bragged about her beauty. The sea god Poseidon wanted to punish her for her pride. He sent a sea monster to destroy her kingdom. The only way to save her people was to **sacrifice** her daughter to the monster. The princess Andromeda was bravely rescued. But Poseidon wanted to be sure Cassiopeia had learned her lesson. He tied her to her **throne**. Then he set her in the sky. He made sure Cassiopeia tipped uncomfortably upside down as she circled the heavens. The outline of the seated queen looks like a *W* in the summer sky. In winter, the constellation Cassiopeia forms an unhappy *M*.

Star Light, Star Bright

Stars are bright globes made of gas. Some are white-hot. Others are slightly cooler. Some appear red or blue. Others are yellow like our Sun. Some stars are the size of cities. Others are giant—many thousands of times larger than Earth. The brightest stars can be seen from trillions of miles away. Cassiopeia has some of the brightest stars in the night sky.

▲ The Sun is the closest star to Earth.

Stars in Cassiopeia

Cassiopeia's *W* is made up of five stars. At the brightest end of the *W* is the white star Caph. Its name describes how the Arabs saw these stars. Instead of a queen, they saw the five fingers of a hand. The first zig in the *W* leads to Shedar. This giant orange star is even brighter than Caph. It sits at Queen Cassiopeia's chest. Gamma Cassiopeiae is the middle star. The next zag leads to Ruchbah. Its name means "knee." The star marks the knee of Cassiopeia. The final and faintest star in the *W* marks Cassiopeia's leg.

▼ Cassiopeia's bright W shape is easy to see if you look for it.

Gamma Cassiopeiae

Ruchbah

Caph

Shedar

Looking Deeper

Cassiopeia's throne is set against the Milky Way. There is something special about this brilliant band of stars and gases. They make up our **galaxy**. The Milky Way galaxy is like a bright disk. We can see only the edge of the disk. It stretches deep into space behind Cassiopeia.

The Milky Way is home to many star clusters. These groups of stars are held close together by **gravity**. There are star clusters in Cassiopeia. They can be seen through a telescope. One cluster is called M52. It is a dense cluster of bluish stars. A line drawn from Shedar through Caph points to it. The M103 cluster near Ruchbah has a huge red star. NGC 7789 is another colorful cluster in Cassiopeia.

SUPERNOVAS

Stars are not living objects. But they still have life cycles. Stars are born in clouds of dust and gases. They burn for billions of years. Some giant stars die in huge explosions called supernovas.
A supernova is blindingly bright and beautiful. The remains of some supernovas can be seen in Cassiopeia. A famous one is Cassiopeia A. This star exploded in the 1600s. A line drawn from Ruchbah through Gamma Cassiopeiae points to it. Little is still visible of Cassiopeia A. But it still sends out lots of X-ray waves and heat.

▶ Opposite page: Our galaxy is the Milky Way.

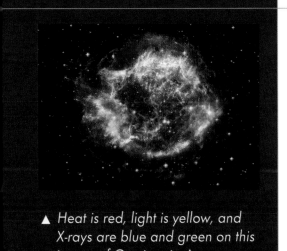

▲ Heat is red, light is yellow, and X-rays are blue and green on this image of Cassiopeia A.

Countless other galaxies lie beyond the Milky Way. Two of them are found in Cassiopeia. The half of the *W* tipped by Shedar points to galaxies called NGC 147 and NGC 185. This small pair of galaxies moves around the larger Andromeda galaxy.

Cassiopeia's Family

Cassiopeia does not tilt through the skies alone. She is surrounded by family. The starry image of her husband, King Cepheus, is forever at her side. Also nearby are her daughter and son-in-law, Andromeda and Perseus. In the Northern **Hemisphere**, watch the sky on winter nights. The constellations of the entire royal family are in view.

Other Constellations

A total of 88 constellations decorate the night sky. Greek **astronomer** Ptolemy wrote a book around the year 150. He described 48 constellations. The other 40 constellations were added in the 1600s and 1700s. In the 1900s, scientists drew official borders around the constellations. They divided the sky into 88 areas with no space in between. This means every star seen from Earth is part of a constellation.

THE THREE GUIDES

The brightest star in Cassiopeia has long been used to help find the North Star, Polaris. People on Earth use Polaris to find the direction north. Along with two stars in the constellations Perseus and Andromeda, Caph is one of the Three Guides. These stars mark an imaginary line that passes through Polaris.

▶ Opposite page: Cassiopeia (in red) sits near the North Star.

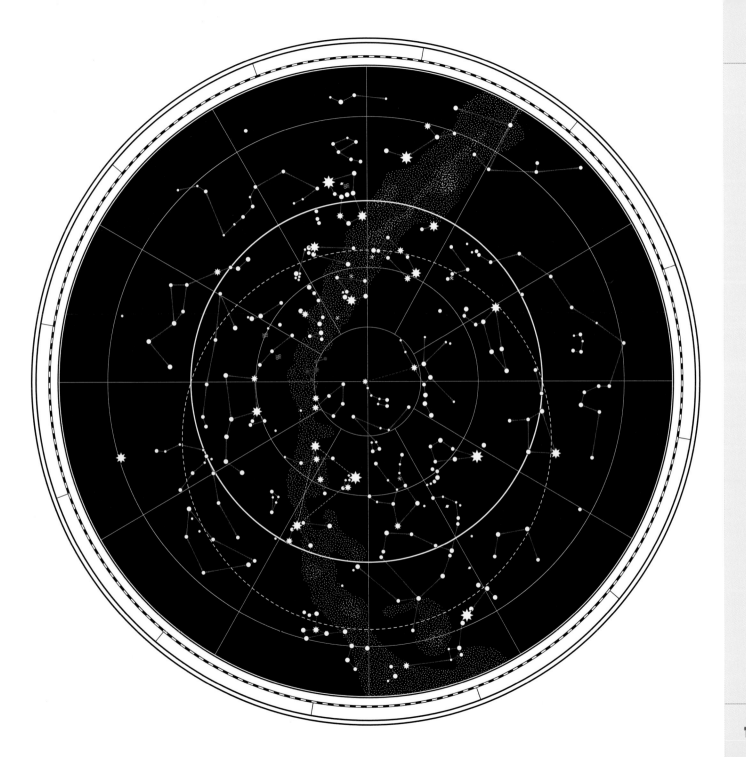

CHAPTER 2

The Origin of the Myth of Cassiopeia

▲ *Ancient tablets mentioned t*
stars in Cassiopeia.

People traced patterns through Cassiopeia's stars long before Ptolemy's time. This constellation is so old that no one knows exactly who first noticed its shape. It may have been known as early as 3500 BC. Most agree the constellation was invented in the ancient Middle East near the Euphrates River. Clay tablets later found in the region describe its stars.

Several ancient cultures recognized the *W* shape of Cassiopeia. Each imagined the stars to represent something different. The Arabs saw a hand, a camel, or a dog. Ancient Egyptians saw a leg in the sky. The Chinese saw horses and a **chariot**. Ancient Greeks saw an early version of a key. The Celts saw the palace of a fairy king. It was not until later that Cassiopeia became a queen.

▼ Ancient people living near the Euphrates River were expert astronomers.

The Unhappy Queen

The ancient Greeks told the story of Queen Cassiopeia. But they likely borrowed her name and parts of her story from another culture. Experts disagree on where the myth of Cassiopeia came from. Some believe it was taken from Middle Eastern culture. Others believe the myth began in India.

Greek astronomer Eudoxus lived in the 300s BC. He was the first Greek known to write about Cassiopeia and other constellations. But his work would be lost if it weren't for the Greek poet Aratus. He made Eudoxus's writing into a poem. This poem is all that survived of Eudoxus's work. Aratus described Cassiopeia as unhappy. He imagined her with her arms spread wide and her head pointed down. Other Greek and Roman writers retold Cassiopeia's story in the following centuries. Some stories say Cassiopeia was from Ethiopia. Some say she was a queen in the Middle East. Each writer told the story just a little bit differently. But the main ideas were always the same.

◄ Opposite page: There are many versions of the story of Cassiopeia.

Cassiopeia in Greek Culture

The story of Cassiopeia served as a lesson for the Greeks. In Greek culture, pride was a serious sin. Cassiopeia was too proud. She placed herself and her daughter above the gods. Greeks believed this kind of pride brought punishment from the gods. Cassiopeia was a perfect example. Her bright stars could always be seen in the night sky. They were a constant reminder to be **humble**.

The story of Cassiopeia's daughter, Andromeda, was also important to the Greeks. Andromeda was an innocent beauty. She almost lost her life because of her mother's vanity.

But the hero Perseus saved her at the last moment. And Perseus instantly fell in love with her. This classic story was very popular among the Greeks. Perseus became a beloved hero in Greece and around the world. Countless artists have painted the daring rescue of Andromeda. Many plays and operas tell the story of Cassiopeia's family.

PERSEUS AND PEGASUS

Perseus was so famous that he eventually replaced another Greek character. The hero Bellerophon was the original rider of the winged horse Pegasus. But many writers and artists liked Perseus better than Bellerophon. In their version of the myth, Perseus rode to Andromeda's rescue on Pegasus.

CHAPTER 3

The Story of Cassiopeia

Cassiopeia was queen of Ethiopia. She was very beautiful, and she was proud of her beauty. Cassiopeia also had a daughter, Andromeda. The lovely Andromeda was engaged to be married. She was even more beautiful than her mother.

Cassiopeia was as proud of Andromeda's beauty as she was of her own. The queen couldn't resist boasting. One day, Cassiopeia's pride got the best of her. She bragged that she and Andromeda were more beautiful even than the sea nymphs, spirits of the ocean.

The vain queen's words drifted over the nearby sea. They soon reached the sea nymphs' ears. The sea nymphs were furious when they heard Cassiopeia! They went to the powerful sea god Poseidon. They told him what the queen had said. Poseidon listened to their words. His anger quickly grew. Finally he could not stand it. He promised to punish Cassiopeia for her vanity.

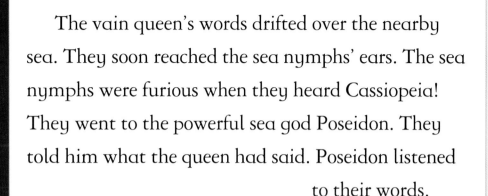

Poseidon sent a fearsome sea monster to destroy Cassiopeia's kingdom. She and King Cepheus were horrified when they learned of this threat. Cepheus knew he had to do something to save his kingdom. He visited an **oracle** for advice. But the advice was

not what Cepheus wanted to hear. The oracle said there was only one way to save their kingdom. They had to sacrifice their only daughter to the hungry sea monster.

Cepheus couldn't bear the thought of Andromeda being eaten. But his people convinced him he had no choice. They forced him to chain Andromeda to a rock pounded by waves. She now lay helplessly in the sea monster's path. It would not be long before the evil creature came and swallowed her. Cepheus and Cassiopeia looked on fearfully. Andromeda wept. There was nothing for her to do now but accept her cruel fate.

Just then, a man flew overhead. Wings on his sandals carried him through the air. His name was Perseus. He was a son of the mighty Zeus, king of the gods. Perseus had just beheaded the snake-haired Medusa. She was so ugly that any who looked at her turned to stone. Perseus was flying home past the kingdom.

Perseus looked down at Andromeda. The weeping princess was too beautiful. He could not leave her. Perseus was in love. He landed near her and asked why she was chained. Andromeda shyly answered. But her words trailed off in a scream. The sea monster's scaly head was rising over the waves.

Perseus quickly flew over to Cassiopeia and Cepheus. He said he would try to rescue their daughter. But he made them promise him something first. If he saved Andromeda, she had to marry him. The king and queen agreed. Just before the monster reached Andromeda, Perseus flew high into the air. The sea monster saw his shadow on the waves. Perseus dove from above as the monster attacked his reflection. He plunged his blade deep into the creature's flesh, cutting off its head.

Perseus gently released Andromeda from her chains. Then it was time to celebrate. A wedding feast was held for Perseus and the princess. But the splendid event was soon spoiled.

Andromeda's ex-fiancé, Agenor, stomped in. He brought his army with him. He ordered Andromeda to marry him instead of Perseus. The princess stayed loyal to Perseus. But Cassiopeia and Cepheus changed their minds. They said Andromeda had been engaged to Agenor first. He should be the one she married. They encouraged Agenor and his army to kill Perseus.

Perseus fought bravely. But he was no match for Agenor's large army. Luckily, Perseus still had Medusa's head. He told the princess to close her eyes. Then he pulled the head out of his bag. He held it up for his enemies to see. Each and every one of them turned to stone. Andromeda and Perseus were finally married. They lived a happy life together.

The gods honored Andromeda's family by placing them in the sky as constellations. But Poseidon was still angry at Cassiopeia. He bound her to her throne. He set her in the sky at an uncomfortable angle. Forever after, she would circle the pole with her head slanted down.

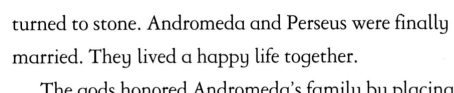

CHAPTER 4

Cassiopeia in Other Cultures

The bright *W* of Cassiopeia has caused wonder since ancient times. Many cultures have woven their own stories around these stars. Early Arabs saw them as the fingertips of a hand painted with henna. Women used this reddish dye to decorate their hands and feet. The designs were beautiful and were believed to bring good luck. Other Arabs saw the humps of a kneeling camel in the constellation. Camels were hugely important in Arab culture. They were transportation and food for many desert peoples.

The Chinese saw the story of chariot driver Wang Liang. Gamma Cassiopeiae was his whip.

▲ Women decorate their hands and feet with henna.

▶ Opposite page: Ancient Chinese armies used horse-drawn chariots in war.

Wang Liang once drove for a hunter. The hunter could not hit a single bird unless Wang Liang cheated by driving too close to them. The hunter offered to hire Wang Liang as his driver full time. But Wang Liang said no. He did not want to drive for a man who would rather cheat than follow the rules.

The Native American Quileute people tell the story of a large elk skin. The stars show through holes made by the stakes used to stretch the skin. The Chukchi of northeastern Russia see five reindeer in the river of the Milky Way.

CHAPTER 5

How to Find Cassiopeia

Cassiopeia is easy to spot in the night sky. She can always be seen from the Northern Hemisphere. To find her, face north. Look for the Little Dipper. The star at the tip of its handle is Polaris. Cassiopeia circles this star. Look nearby in the Milky Way for her *W* shape in summer. She will appear high in the sky as an *M* in winter.

Another useful trick is to look for the familiar Big Dipper. It always sits across from Cassiopeia on the other side of Polaris. Trace a line from any star on the Big Dipper's handle through Polaris. This line is sure to point to Cassiopeia.

THE PERSEID METEOR SHOWER
Each August, shooting stars whiz through the constellation Cassiopeia. These shooting stars aren't really stars at all. They are meteors. Their bright streaks are seen when small rocks from space pass too close to Earth. The Perseid meteor shower is one of the best times to see meteors. They shoot out from a point between Cassiopeia and Perseus. On some August nights, up to 50 meteors flash through the sky every hour.

▶ *Opposite page: Cassiopeia tilts upside down as she circles Polaris.*

Glossary

astronomer (uh-STRAW-nuh-mur)
A scientist who studies stars and other objects in space is called an astronomer. The astronomer discovered a new star.

chariot (CHAR-ee-uht)
A chariot is a small vehicle pulled by horses. The stars tell the story of Chinese chariot driver Wang Liang.

galaxy (GAL-ax-ee)
A group of millions or billions of stars form a galaxy. Our galaxy is called the Milky Way.

gravity (GRAV-uh-tee)
Gravity is a force that pulls objects toward each other. Gravity pulls stars together.

hemisphere (HEM-uh-spheer)
One half of a planet is one hemisphere. You can see Cassiopeia from the Northern Hemisphere.

humble (HUM-buhl)
A person who is humble is not proud and does not feel more important than others. Zeus wanted Cassiopeia to be more humble.

oracle (OR-uh-kuhl)
An oracle is a person who speaks for the gods. The oracle gave advice to King Cepheus.

sacrifice (SAK-ruh-fise)
To sacrifice is to give up something of value for the sake of something more important. Cassiopeia was going to sacrifice her daughter to the sea monster.

throne (THROHN)
A throne is the chair of a queen or king. Cassiopeia's throne tips upside down in the sky.

universe (YOU-nih-verse)
The universe is everything that exists in space. The universe is huge and filled with stars.

vain (VAYN)
A vain person is very proud, especially of his or her appearance. Cassiopeia was vain.

Learn More

Books

Napoli, Donna Jo. *Treasury of Greek Mythology: Classic Stories of Gods, Goddesses, Heroes, and Monsters.* Washington, DC: National Geographic, 2011.

Rey, H. A. *Find the Constellations.* Boston: Houghton Mifflin, 2008.

Sparrow, Giles. *Night Sky.* New York: Scholastic, 2013.

Web Sites

Visit our Web site for links about Cassiopeia:

childsworld.com/links

Note to Parents, Teachers, and Librarians:
We routinely verify our Web links to make sure they are safe and active sites.
So encourage your readers to check them out!

Index